ashley bryan

words to my life's song

by ashley bryan

with photographs by bill mcguinness

atheneum books for young readers: new york london toronto sydney

Atheneum Books for Young Readers

An imprint of Simon & Schuster Children's Publishing Division
1230 Avenue of the Americas, New York, New York 10020

Book design by Michael McCartney
The text for this book is set in Lucian BT and Chaparral Pro.

Manufactured in China
First Edition * 10 9 8 7 6 5 4 3 2 1

Library of Congress Cataloging-in-Publication Data

Bryan, Ashley.
Ashley Bryan : words to my life's song / by Ashley Bryan. — 1st ed. * p.   cm.

1. Bryan, Ashley—Juvenile literature. 2. Authors, American—20th century—Biography—Juvenile literature.
3. African American authors—Biography—Juvenile literature. 4. Children's stories—Authorship—Juvenile literature.

5. African American illustrators—Biography—Juvenile literature. 6. African American artists—Biography—Juvenile literature. I. Title.
ISBN-13: 978-1-4169-0541-7 * ISBN-10: 1-4169-0541-3

PS3552.R848Z46 2009
818'.54—dc21   [B] 2008014369

To the memory of my sister,
Ernestine Bryan Haskins, 1925–2008.
And for my family, and to the earth, the sky,
the sea that make all of us one family.

I cannot remember a time when I have not been drawing and painting.

In an early photo of my family, I am sitting on my mother's lap. My older brother, Sidney, stands with a bag in his hand. If you put a paintbrush in my hand, that would best complete the picture.

The morning sun jewels the dewdrops on the grass.
Walk with me on this Maine island where I now live
as I tell my story. Down the road is a sandy beach
lined with boathouses. I have a sketch pad in hand.

I was the second of six children—four boys and two girls—growing up in the Bronx in New York City. We lived in walk-up apartment buildings, four or five stories high. The apartments were called "railroad apartments" because they went in a straight line from one room to the other. There was a window overlooking the street, an air shaft in the middle, and a fire escape on the back window. In good weather we often sat on the fire escape. It was the Depression era. Wandering musicians performed in the backyard. We'd wrap a few spare coins in newspaper and toss them down in thanks. When I was twelve, three cousins came to live with us when their mother died. It was like getting three new siblings!

Yes, it was quite a crowd. But my mother made our apartment so beautiful that everyone enjoyed visiting. She loved flowers, and wherever there was light, there was a plant. Where there was no light, she made colorful crepe paper flowers to brighten the shadowed areas. We children spun green paper strands around the wire stems that held the flower heads. My parents saw how much I loved drawing and painting and helping with the flowers, so one day they brought home a small desk with cubbyholes and drawers for my artwork and materials. I'd sit at that desk in the corner while my brothers and sisters would be dancing to the music of popular songs and playing games of checkers, tiddlywinks, or pick-up sticks, laughing and chatting all the while.

Sometimes I'd join in, but usually I'd draw away into my private world as if I were in my own quiet studio.

During the Great Depression, people were poor, but the government offered free art and music classes across the country. My parents sent us out to these WPA (Works Progress Administration) classes saying, "Learn to entertain yourselves." And we did. We drew, we painted, and we played musical instruments. I remember the art teacher, Mr. Margolis, who introduced us to the work of the Impressionist artists, which opened a whole new world of working in color for me. Like most children I started by painting a red apple a solid red. Now I began to play with contrasting colors to enhance the red of the apple.

We walk the beach, small figures in the open space of sky and sea. Before us the tide rolls in. Each expiring wave brings new treasures. We look across the ocean to a distant island. Boats at anchor sway on their moorings. Bright yellow goldfinches hop in and out of the rosebushes that line the shore.

My dad loved birds. Our living room was lined with shelves for birdcages. At one time I counted over one hundred birds: canaries, finches, warblers, parakeets. My mother would say, "If I want any attention around here, I'd have to get into a cage!"

My mother sang from one end of the day to the other. When childhood friends visited, they would say, "Your mother sings!" I thought all mothers sang. My dad would say, "Your mother must think she's a bird."

Although we used our apartment space well, my dad promised that one day we'd get our own private house. "Sidney will have his own room, Ashley and Ernie will have their own rooms." "Oh, Daddy, Daddy, Daddy!" we'd exclaim, hopping up and down, thinking it would happen that very next week. However, it wasn't until the Second World War, when we nine children were grown, that a private house across the street put up a FOR SALE sign. My dad immediately went over there and made a down payment. My dad was so proud of this house that when people said to him, "I love your gray, shingled house!" he'd say, "Oh no, that's not gray. It's heather!" I'd sit by the window of my room, playing the guitar or drawing from the familiar scene of my neighbors across the street, congregated on the stoop and sidewalk of the apartment building in which we once lived.

The seagulls flying above us remind me of my father's birds. Occasionally one of his birds would escape the cage and wing its way through the apartment. We'd chase after the bird while cheering it in flight.

The seagulls, however, soar free.

My parents were

born in Antigua,

in the British West Indies. They had been childhood sweethearts. Soon after World War I, they immigrated to the United States and were married in New York City. My mother would say, "If I hadn't married your father, I'd never have married!"

In the English colonies, many young people were apprenticed to a trade as part of their schooling. My dad was apprenticed to the printing trade. Yet at his first job in a downtown New York building, he was given a mop and a broom. He didn't tell us about the prevailing racial discrimination that limited job opportunities for colored people. He instead told us jokingly, "How could I concentrate on the mop and broom with all those pretty legs going by?" Still he was determined to get a job in his trade, so he went to the British consulate and got a letter stating that he was a veteran of World War I. This led to a job with Marrano and Bellini, printers in downtown New York. For me, the best part was that he'd bring home a variety of papers left over from printing orders. I had so much to choose from for my artwork. When the Depression ended the demand for the special work of these printers, my dad set up his own little printing shop. **More paper!**

11

Over a stony rise of the shore, we come down to a sweeping curve of a pebbly beach. In the distance is a small island topped with a lighthouse, a signal of caution to avoid the surrounding rocky shoals.

I published my very first book in kindergarten. As we learned the alphabet, we drew pictures for each letter. When we reached the letter *Z*, the teacher gave us colored paper to make a cover for our alphabet pictures. We sewed the pages together and the teacher said, "You have just published an alphabet book. You are the author, illustrator, and binder. Take it home." We became the distributors as well. After the alphabet book, we made number books, word books, books of whatever we learned. I got hugs, kisses, and applause from family and friends for these books. The teacher called these "rave reviews," and this inspired me to make gifts of books ever since.

The local elementary school that I attended was PS 2. This school was an amazing mix of languages and cultures—Black, Irish, Italian, German, Polish, and Jewish. I loved hearing the different languages and seeing the different things other children drew. These children were my classmates and friends from elementary school through high school.

There was something else I loved about school. From the earliest grades, PS 2 taught the practice of performing poetry. We would select a poem and practice it for weeks. Each morning, class would begin with poetry recitations by two or three students. This understanding of poetry as a performance art has never left me. It is at the heart of all my work.

Let's slow down and choose
from the tide-smoothed stones,
some for our pockets and
some to offer to others.
Later I'll take you to my
favorite beach for collecting
stones. We'll also select
seashells, bones, driftwood,
and sea glass as we go.

16

When we were growing up, my mother read to us stories from the Bible. There was a big church next door to our school. Its stained-glass windows glowed. Its bells rang on Sunday mornings. We said, "Mama, we want to go to that big pretty church." So one Sunday my mother took us to this church, St. John's Evangelical Lutheran Church on Fulton Avenue and 169th Street in the Bronx. When I was a boy, the church held services in English and in German. The Sunday school superintendent, Mr. George Wedemeyer, welcomed us and we became the first Black family to join that church. Pins were given annually for perfect attendance to the children and teachers of the Sunday school. The first year was a circle pin, then a wreath around the circle was added for the second year. After that, colorful bars indicating the years of perfect attendance were added to the pin. I began earning my perfect-attendance pins. I admired our teachers coming forward year after year, earning their bars for ten, fifteen, twenty years of perfect attendance.

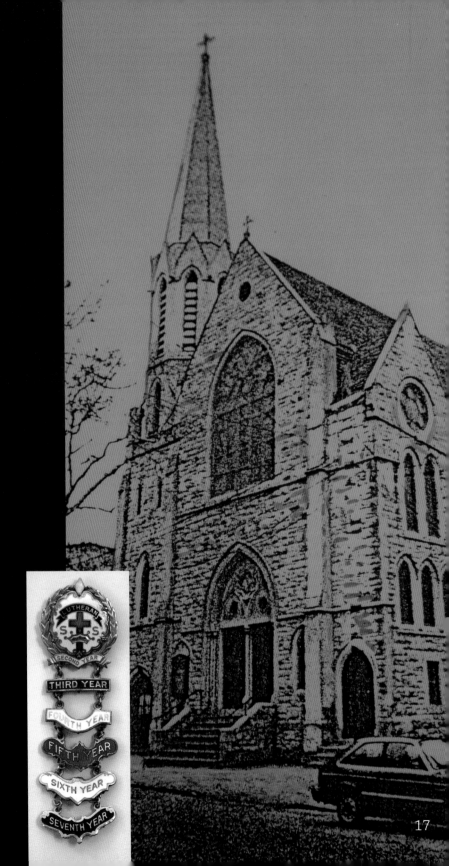

the bright, blessed day,

the dark, sacred night,

A shower! Never mind. And see, now a rainbow arches its band of colors from the mountains to the ocean. No matter how often I see this, I gasp in wonder, time and time again.

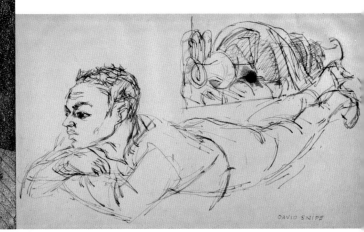

DAVID SNIPE

I was sixteen when I graduated from Theodore Roosevelt High School in the Bronx, but I could not go to college without a scholarship. With portfolio in hand, I was interviewed at one of the leading art institutes. The interviewer stated that mine was the best portfolio that he had seen. However, he also informed me that it would be a waste to give a scholarship to a colored person.

I remembered my parents saying that if you are doing something creative and constructive, don't let anyone or anything ever stop you. I did not give up. I was able to take a postgraduate program in my high school and was advised to apply to the Cooper Union School of Art and Engineering the following summer. "They do not see you there," my art teachers said, encouraging me. In 1940 the Cooper Union entrance exam was in three parts: drawing, architecture, and sculpture. When completed, we set our exam responses in a tray with our names and addresses. The trays were placed on the platform of the Great Hall and we left. Since the evaluators literally did not see us, there was no way to determine the race of the applicants. I was fortunate to be accepted to the art school, which was tuition free, and still is. I was the only Black in my class—in fact, all through those school years, I had always been one of the few Blacks in my classes. I had learned early to focus on my love of my studies. Now I was excited to pursue my studies in art. At the Cooper Union, I could take courses in sculpture, calligraphy, design, book illustration, and painting. Painting became my great favorite.

The Bronx community no longer reflects the diverse ethnic backgrounds of the people with whom I grew up. Today the population is predominately Black and Hispanic. I still maintain my membership with St. John's Evangelical Lutheran Church, which stands today. In the 1990s a fire started in the church vestry. Fortunately, it was stopped at the altar. However, a major stained-glass window over the altar was destroyed. The church contacted me to design a replacement for the Resurrection window. All of the images in the existing stained-glass windows of the church pictured Caucasians in the scenes of the life of Jesus. For the replacement window I designed a Black Jesus rising from the tomb. A noted stained-glass studio implemented my design. This window now takes its place with the others.

There!
A glint of blue sea glass.

Broken bottles, rolled and
smoothed, now smooth
in our hand, remind me
of those stained-glass
windows of my childhood.

23

During the Depression, children

often made their own toys. They made soap-box wagons with old carriage wheels, scooters with boards and skates. And so did I. Walking the streets, I'd pick up cast-off materials. I loved the challenge of finding ways of creating new forms from the pieces collected. It was like putting together a puzzle. A favorite thing to do with my sister Ernestine was to gather fabric-sample books that had been discarded by upholstery stores. I would draw patterns of quilts, skirts, and vests that my sister would sew together with the newfound cloth. We'd also help my dad make kites of intriguing shapes—squares, rectangles, boxes—out of vibrantly colored crepe paper, which we flew in the nearby park. Children crowded around us and asked to buy them. Soon we had an additional source of family income!

Here's the town dock and the mail boat, our year-round connection to the mainland. The fishermen's co-op is next to the town dock. Early mornings, you'll see lobstermen sliding crates of fish bait down ramps, loading them onto their boats.

The inspiration that comes from collecting things has stayed with me my whole life. From the child who rescued stray objects from the streets grew the adult who gathers seashells, driftwood, bones, rocks, and sea glass. Sea glass especially—I have jars and jars of it. As my sea-glass collection grew, I felt challenged to find a way to join the pieces together, hold them together in the shape of a ball, a star, or a flower. Since sea glass is irregular in shape, in thickness and thinness, I couldn't take the traditional stained-glass approach. I couldn't use lead tracks, which require flat glass to fit the tracks for soldering. So I experimented with papier-mâché. I soaked newspaper, pounded it to a clayey pulp, then added paste to the pulp. I set the sea-glass pieces on tinfoil and connected the pieces with this pulp. When the mâché dried, I peeled the tinfoil away and the mâché held the pieces together. When held to the light, the pieces glowed like stained glass.

After making simple forms, I decided to make a small panel, twelve inches wide by fourteen inches tall, of a scene from the life of Jesus. I drew

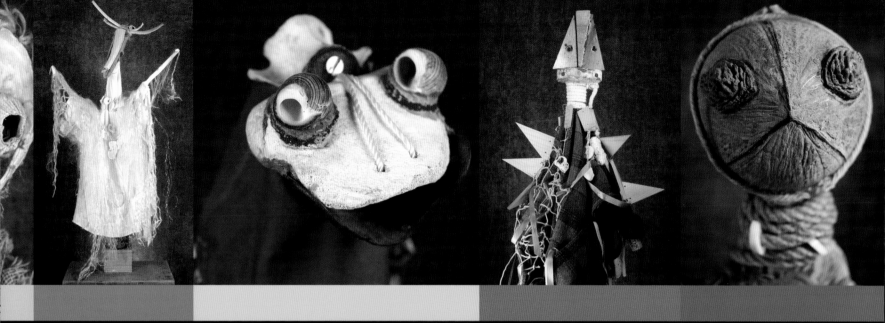

a design, covered it with translucent wax paper, then followed the design with glass pieces, holding them together with papier-mâché. When the panel dried, I reinforced the back with more mâché, and then painted it black. Held to the light, this panel was like a medieval stained-glass window. This led to my series of glass panels on the life of Jesus.

At the same time, I began creating masklike heads from the bones, driftwood, and shells that I'd collected. These became the hand puppets, a repertory company of actors for staging my African folktale plays for the islanders.

Now we're back at my home. Here are my puppets and the sea-glass panels. When you can see the promise in discarded things, you can make more of whatever you touch. I've always sought to create something useful, something beautiful, with objects that have been cast-off, disregarded.

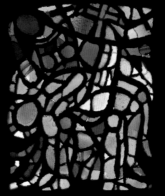

I was seventeen when

I began my studies at Cooper Union. Two years later I was drafted into the army to serve in World War II. The army was segregated, and Black troops were generally assigned into service units. My assignment was to handle cargo, mainly at docks, with the 270 Port Company, 502 Port Battalion. A number of the men in the company had worked as stevedores. I knew nothing of dockwork. Nevertheless, I was given the position of winch operator and graded as a tech sergeant, T4. On the basis of IQ ratings I was also asked to attend Officer Candidate School. I refused. I had no ambitions about rank and was determined to stay with the men I had come to know. After basic training at Camp Myles Standish, in Taunton, Massachusetts, we were assigned to work at the dockyards in Boston and were housed in a schoolhouse in South Boston.

The neighborhood children were very curious about us soldiers and often came to visit, sometimes walking the post with me when I was on guard duty. When I had days off, I brought art materials into the schoolyard and they'd come and draw with me. I missed them when our battalion sailed overseas to Scotland and even wrote them letters as I continued doing dockwork at the port of Glasgow.

Black soldiers were often restricted to the barracks after work, to keep us from fraternizing with the White community. I'd heard that there was an art school in Glasgow, and so I asked the battalion commander, Colonel Pierce, for permission to attend the Glasgow School of Art when I was not on duty. Some of the students became friends.

They invited me to their homes and churches and to theatrical events. At the Cooper Union in New York, we drew from live models. We were inspired by the impact of African art from the turn of the century on avant-garde European art. At the Glasgow School of Art, the students drew from plaster casts of Greek and Roman statues, formal drawings carefully rendered. I surprised my classmates with my swift sketches and exaggerated proportions of the body.

All through the war years, I drew whenever I could. I kept a sketch pad and art supplies in my gas mask. There would have been a tumble of materials if I were ever in need of that mask! During any lull, I would take out my sketch pad and draw. I had great respect for the men in my unit and they supported my artwork. Because I was so inept at the winch, they often took over my winch operation post and said, "Ashley, you draw!" I also wrote lots of letters. Letters were reduced to a small size called V-mail. My Cooper Union friend, Eva Brussel, saved my war correspondences and recently sent them to me. What a gift to be able to reacquaint myself with that nineteen-year-old young man!

In June 1944, we left Glasgow in the fleet that sailed for Normandy, France, and took part in the invasion, the June 6 surprise landing on Omaha Beach. Barrage balloons floated overhead to distract the bombers, but on a ship loaded with backup supplies, ammunition crates among them, it was a fearful time. There was a great loss of life before the beachhead was secured. Still, we pressed forward. Our secret weapon was a newly created vessel that was a boat on the water and a truck on land, the amphibious "duck." We unloaded our cargo onto the ducks and went ashore, walking gingerly, hoping to avoid land mines, and dug our foxholes. But on that first day, I couldn't tighten the joint of my collapsible shovel. It kept closing up on me. I dug down barely twelve inches by the time the evening strafing from enemy planes started up, but I felt I had room to spare as I flattened out in the shallow space. The next day one of my friends enlarged his foxhole and took me in.

There are words like **F**reedom
Sweet and wonderful to say.
On my heart-strings freedom sings
All day everyday.

LANGSTON HUGHES

I'm **P**aula the cat
not thin nor fat
as happy as house cats can be

But now I've the urge
for my spirit to surge
and I shall go off
to sea

NIKKI GIOVANNI

Harriet Tubman didn't take no stuff
Wasn't scared of nothing neither
Didn't come in this world to be no slave
And wasn't going to stay one either

ELOISE GREENFIELD

We'll watch our step as we walk this Little Cranberry beach, not because of any danger, but so as not to miss those rocks that we cannot live without. Offshore, lobstermen at their marked buoys are hauling the lobster traps. They check the catch to determine what may be kept and what will be thrown back into the ocean. The seagulls hover, ready to swoop down at discarded bait and scraps. The lobstermen's round of traps completes their day.

The war ended.

My unit was terribly eager to finally go home. But the 270 Port Company did not return home as a unit as other units had. Because of the segregation on ships, there were only a few places for Black soldiers on each boat's homeward journey. We left France in dribbles of small, dispirited groups at a time. But once home, I was very happy and grateful to complete my studies at the Cooper Union. That was in 1946, the year that the Skowhegan School of Painting and Sculpture in central Maine was founded. The school awarded scholarships to art schools across the country to pull in the strongest artists. I was one of two students at Cooper Union granted a summer scholarship. That summer of painting from the Maine landscape opened a whole new direction for me. I also learned the art of fresco there. We'd prepare a mixture of sand, plaster, and lime, which we spread on the wall. We then mixed dry pigments with water, and applied that onto the damp wall. When the wall dried, the color was fixed permanently—a wonderful thing!

Weekends I often visited Acadia National Park. From Cadillac Mountain I saw the beautiful Cranberry islands off the coast. The Cranberry Isles would become my annual summer retreat, my most intensive time, devoted entirely to painting. But that was all to come. I had experienced so much of the sufferings of war and the tragedies of people caught in the war that I could not go straight on as a painter. Questions haunted me, especially, "Why does Man, knowing the overwhelming tragedies of war, choose war?" I needed to find out. When I returned from Skowhegan, I enrolled as an undergraduate at Columbia University, majoring in philosophy. Although there were no answers to my questions, I was intrigued by systems of thought. I stayed with the challenge and completed my undergraduate studies as a philosophy major.

The seasons describe
this island.

Spring

summer

autumn

winter . . .

Some days, in any season,
we walk in fog so thick,
so deep, we can scarcely
see what lies ahead.

But I didn't lose my need for and love of painting. During my years at Columbia I made appointments with publishers to show my art portfolio. Early in 1947, I met with Kurt and Helen Wolff, founders of Pantheon Books, and who were putting together a book of African tales. They were immediately struck by the artwork that I had done for *Aesop's Fables* in Cooper Union. They felt that this approach would be ideal for the art of the book. As each tale was completed, it was sent to me for illustration. Every few months I would bring in the art I was doing. They were ecstatic! By the time of my 1950 graduation from Columbia, I had completed all of the art for this project—over thirty paintings in black and white and red and beige, and fifty black-and-white paintings, all in tempera (poster paints).

After Columbia, I decided to devote myself to my work as an artist. I sailed for southern France to continue my art education under the GI Bill. The GI Bill, under the Department of Veteran's Affairs, paid for further educational studies for all veterans. In Aix-en-Provence, I enrolled at the Université d'Aix-Marseille and studied French but spent most of the time painting. It was right at the time when the great cellist, Pablo Casals, persuaded by his great musician friends, agreed to break his silence (a protest over the Franco regime in his native Spain) to honor the two hundredth anniversary of the death of Bach. Casals lived in exile in the small Catalan town of Prades. He held a series of concerts in the great Baroque cathedral there. Musician friends came from all over the world to join him in honoring the great composer.

Here's our island church, for people of all religious backgrounds. It houses a small organ renovated and installed by the renowned organ builder, Fisk. A week of concerts were given to the islanders by leading organists in celebration.

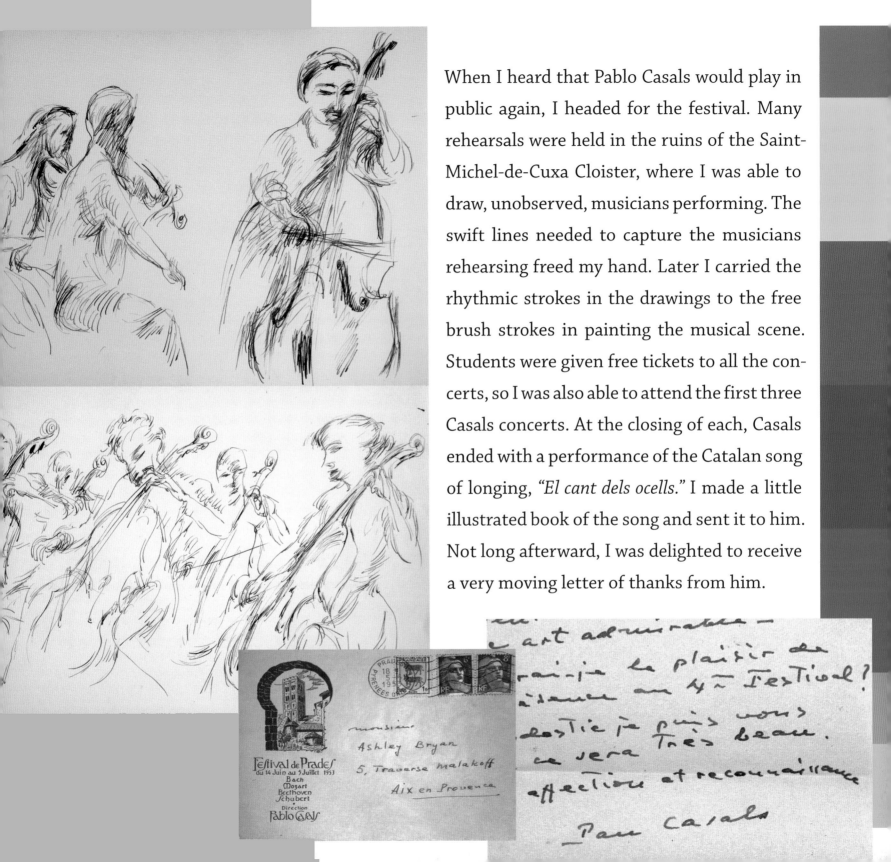

When I heard that Pablo Casals would play in public again, I headed for the festival. Many rehearsals were held in the ruins of the Saint-Michel-de-Cuxa Cloister, where I was able to draw, unobserved, musicians performing. The swift lines needed to capture the musicians rehearsing freed my hand. Later I carried the rhythmic strokes in the drawings to the free brush strokes in painting the musical scene. Students were given free tickets to all the concerts, so I was also able to attend the first three Casals concerts. At the closing of each, Casals ended with a performance of the Catalan song of longing, *"El cant dels ocells."* I made a little illustrated book of the song and sent it to him. Not long afterward, I was delighted to receive a very moving letter of thanks from him.

During the summer I paint outdoors. Ah, the irises are in bloom. I'll stop and paint them, you go relax. When people see my paintings on exhibit, they often ask, "Did you paint these in Antigua?" They think only of the gray and rockbound Maine coast but are not aware of the riotous blossoming Maine gardens sport throughout their short flowering season.

While I was in France I received news from Pantheon Books that the Bollingen Foundation had bought the rights to Paul Radin's book of African tales and had decided to use photographs of African sculpture and masks to accompany the text. The Wolffs were sorry that my imaginative illustrations could not be used. So was I. The possible opening to what had been my entry into the book field closed. It would be many years before that door opened again.

When I returned to the Bronx in 1953, I began working full-time, teaching art. I taught in many schools, including the Dalton's Lower School, before leaving the children for adults at Queens College. I used whatever time I had after work to paint in my studio. However, I continued to spend summers on the Cranberry Isles. In 1956, I returned to Skowhegan. I had won the annual competition to paint a fresco in the South Solon Free Meeting House. Each year an artist was selected to paint one of the walls in this meetinghouse until all the walls were frescoed. I decorated a curved back wall behind the central pews; my theme was the parable of the sower. Recently, I returned for the fiftieth-anniversary celebration of the frescoes painted at the meetinghouse. The frescoes looked as fresh as they had the day they were painted.

I returned home, longing to continue to be able to give all of my day to developing as a painter. So I applied for a Fulbright grant and was fortunate in receiving the award of a Fulbright scholarship to Germany. I became a student at the University of Freiburg im Breisgau, in southern Germany, and studied German. I had always loved the poetry of Rainer Maria Rilke and had read it at home in German-English translations. I'd even memorized English versions of my favorites. I brought these bilingual books with me to Germany and worked through German poetry to get a grasp of the rhythms of that language. (After almost fifty years those poems, in German, are still vivid in memory.) And, as always, I painted. I sketched in the marketplace that formed each day around the Freiburg Cathedral and later painted from these drawings in my room. I became so absorbed in painting the marketplace scenes that I applied for a renewal of the scholarship and was able to stay in Germany for a second year.

Let's join the Fourth of July picnic on the town field. The island's year-round population of eighty people swells to over four hundred with summer cottages occupied, so we have wonderful celebrations. Later in July we'll join the Maypole dance.

Upon my return from Germany, I rented a studio on Tremont Avenue in the Bronx. From my windows I'd draw children playing when the streets were closed off at noon recess. (Many of my drawings for *The Dancing Granny* were based on these drawings.) My younger sister Emerald's five children attended a public school near my studio. My parents had taken Emerald and her children into their home when her marriage ended. I pitched in to help. The children came by after school and I drew and painted them. They ran around the studio and I was always calling,

"Come back! Come back! Come back to the pose!"

I began teaching art again, and a major portion of my earnings went to supporting the children. Their posing for me balanced with my care of them.

47

Let's cut through these woods.

Just beyond that aisle of trees, you'll come to my favorite cove. From the rising mound of boulders a gathering of cormorants stretch and air their wings. Across the ocean the mountains of Acadia National Park on Mount Desert Island line the shore. Take it all in! And below us look down and choose from the varied shapes and colors of stones, treasured stories of the millennia.

In 1962, Jean Karl, an editor at Atheneum publishers, heard of my work and came to my studio in the Bronx. She enjoyed the oil paintings of my family, but she kept returning to the table with my book projects—*Aesop's Fables*, Mother Goose rhymes, and the African folktales that I'd created for the Wolffs at Pantheon. She was excited by the different styles I used to illustrate the various texts. I told her that I was inspired by the cultures of the world and celebrated those influences in my work. Soon after she left my studio, she sent me a contract to begin a project for her. Our first book was a collection of poems by Rabindranath Tagore, *Moon, for What Do You Wait?* Now my books would no longer be one of a kind but printed in the thousands! For my next book project, Jean asked to use my African folktale illustrations that had so impressed her in my studio. I told her that those illustrations were done from documented texts that preserved the story motif but had little relation to the oral tradition of African storytelling. But Jean was determined. "So, Ashley, tell the stories in your own words," she told me.

To get the spirit of the oral tradition for my writing, I practiced reading aloud from the Black American poets, from Paul Laurence Dunbar to Langston Hughes to Nikki Giovanni. I then retold the African tales using the good ideas from poetry in my writing. I hoped this would open the ear to the sound of the voice in the printed word, so that even when reading my stories silently, readers would hear the voice of a storyteller.

And that led to my retelling of African tales. For my Langston Hughes *Carol of the Brown King* tempera paintings, my inspiration was French illuminated manuscripts. The block-print illustrations for my first book of spirituals, *Walk Together Children*, and for *I'm Going to Sing* were inspired by the early religious block printed books. And folk art inspired the watercolors I created for *The Night Has Ears*, a collection of African proverbs. As years went by, I used the money I earned teaching and making books to help my sister Emerald raise her children. I continued this support until they were grown and on their own. No sooner had this happened when the newly established art department at Dartmouth College in Hanover, New Hampshire, invited me to teach. I worked closely with students at Dartmouth at all levels of drawing, painting, and design. During this time my book work increased, and I was frequently invited to give talks about my books. In the late eighties I decided to leave Dartmouth and, finally, give all of my time to my own work. It was then that I chose to make the Cranberry Isles rather than New York City my year-round home.

After many books together, Jean Karl suddenly became ill in the winter of 1999 and died a year later. For almost a year I put my book projects aside. I focused on my painting outdoors. I painted huge canvases of the flowers from my garden. I also worked on sea-glass panels and puppets created from beach finds. Then my new editor at Atheneum, Caitlyn Dlouhy, persuaded me to bring in the stories I had been working on with Jean Karl. We selected *Beautiful Blackbird*, and when she saw my first double-paged spreads in collage, a medium I'd not yet used in my books, she encouraged me to create all of the art for *Beautiful Blackbird* out of cut paper.

I love painting outdoors from the landscape, when weather permits. Later in the day I return to my studio and work on my book projects. At times I turn to work on a puppet or a glass panel. Each activity taps into a different level of energy that allows me to extend my working day. I don't regard visits of family and friends as interruptions. Everything feeds into the day, which feels big here. In response to the flow of events, I hope to validate time, my life.

51

Ashley Bryan's ABC
of **African American**
· **POETRY** ·

CLIMBING JACOB'S LADDER

Heroes of the Bible in African-American Spirituals

"The songs leap off the page, demanding to be played and sung." —*School Library*

ALL NIGHT, ALL DA

*A Child's First Book
of African-American Spirituals*

BEAUTIFUL BLACKBIRD

Beat the Story-Drum, Pum-Pum

by ASHLEY BRYAN

Carol OF THE
Brown Kin

Nativity Poems by **Langston Hu**

I'M GOING TO SING

BLACK AMERICAN SPIRITUALS, Volume Two

Illustrated with his
Coretta Scott King
Award-winning art

ASHLEY BRYAN'S
AFRICAN TALES,
UH-HUH

The
CAT'S
PURR

JETHRO
and the JUMBIE
Susan Cooper

illustrated by Ashley Bryan

Let it Shine

by the Coretta Scott King
Award winner of
Beautiful Blackbird

The Story of
Lightning & Thunder

The Ox of the
Wonderful Horns
and Other
African Folktales

Ashley Bryan

ASHLEY BRYAN

ON
AND THE
TRICH
ICKS

AND ILLUSTRATED BY ASHLEY BRYAN

TURTLE KNOWS
YOUR NAME

Retold and illustrated by
ASHLEY BRYAN

THE NIGHT ASHLEY
BRYAN
African
Proverbs HAS EARS

WHAT A
WONDERFUL WORLD

illustrated by ASHLEY BRYAN

WALK TOGETHER CHILDREN
BLACK AMERICAN SPIRITUALS

WHAT A
MORNING!
The Christmas Story in Black Spirituals

by George David Weiss and Bob Thiele

I was the first in my family to visit Antigua. Although relatives had visited Antigua with their children, my family had not. I stayed with the family of my mother's brother. His home was near the open marketplace of St. John's. I'd sit by the window, and draw and paint from the scene. The features of the people continually reminded me of my family at home. Drawings from the tropical landscape later became the basis for the illustrations in my African tales. I'd also always spend hours on the many fine beaches and in the cool sea.

My parents had not planned to return to Antigua. But as they neared retirement age, I urged them to visit. They made the trip and were happy to have returned. My uncle, who built houses, offered them land that he owned on a hill outside the main town of St. John's. My parents sent the money so that he could build the house that became their permanent home. That freed them to retire. Once there, my parents reveled in the climate and the view from the verandah: the coming and going of cruise ships, freight ships, and small craft in the bay. My mother could now indulge her love of plants. The ground surrounding the house became a glorious garden with mango, coconut palm, and citrus trees as well. My parents have since died and are buried in Antigua. The family house remains, overlooking the harbor. I return regularly to the island, always with my sister Elaine, who is a great cook.

It's evening. I've enjoyed walking the island with you, telling my story. My studio window gives us a perfect view of the sunset moving from one breathtaking moment to another as the first stars appear. The night continues as the day had—full of possibility.

I was in my early twenties when I came to the Cranberry Isles and when I visited my family's home island of Antigua. For over fifty years these islands have inspired my work.

I love encouraging children and adults to make art almost as much as I love making art myself. Teaching art began early for me. I was in my teens when the church I attended gave me the room and materials for art classes, saying, "You have a talent. Share your gifts with others."

And I have tried to do so ever since!

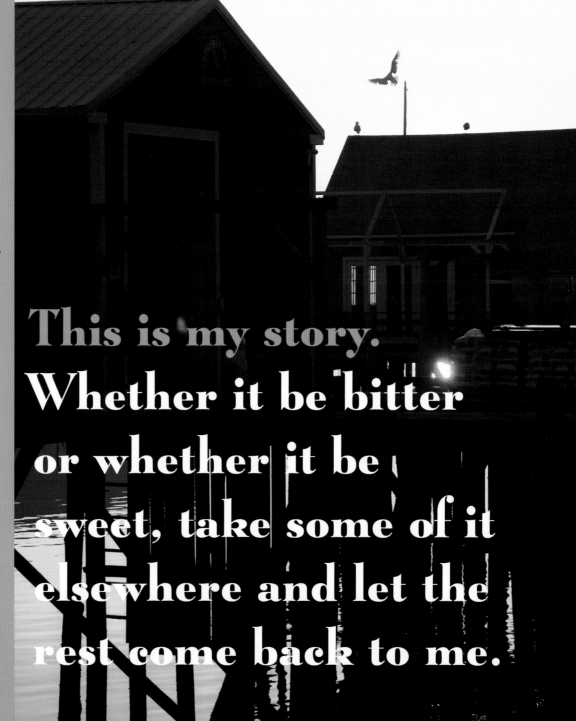

The Ashanti tribe have a saying they use to end their African tales, which is just right for me to close mine with:

This is my story. Whether it be bitter or whether it be sweet, take some of it elsewhere and let the rest come back to me.

Notes on the images

All photographs, unless otherwise noted, are by Bill McGuinness.

p. vi: In my studio, painting
p. 1: Family photograph by Ms. Dunia
p. 3: Paintings of my family made at ages thirteen to fourteen
p. 4: Garden painting, *detail* (*left* and *right*); photograph (*center*) with me (*left*), brothers Donald (*right*) and Ernest (*middle*) with Mama
p. 6: *Deep River*, from *Walk Together Children: The Black American Spirituals*
p. 7: *Do Lord Remember Me*, from *I'm Going to Sing*
p. 8: Photograph of me by Emily Nelligan
pp. 10–11: Photograph of Ma and Dad by Emily Nelligan; WW II painting, Port Battalion, signalman
pp. 12–13: From *Ashley Bryan's African Tales, Uh-Huh*
p. 15: Me, printing a block
p. 17: St. John's Evangelical Lutheran Church, Bronx, New York; perfect-attendance pins (*inset*).
pp. 18–19: From *What a Wonderful World*
p. 21: Benjamin Franklin J.H.S. poetry recitation award; etching, The Cooper Union Art School; WW II drawing
p. 22: St. John's stained-glass window made from my design
p. 23: Holding up a small sea-glass panel, 12" × 14"
p. 24: Toy collection; vest (*inset*) by my sister Ernestine
p. 26: Small sea-glass panels (*background*)
pp. 26–27: Puppets made from beach finds
p. 28: Sea-glass panels of Matthew (man, *left*), Mark (lion, *right*), both 4' × 6'
p. 29: Sea-glass panels of Luke (ox, *left*), John (eagle, *right*), both 4' × 6'
p. 30: Stevedore, WW II drawing; V-mail from WW II
p. 31: Stevedore, WW II drawing, *detail*
p. 32: From *The Story of Lightning & Thunder*
p. 33: From *Ashley Bryan's ABC of African American Poetry*
p. 35: Photograph of me at age twenty-three
p. 37: African tales, unpublished

pp. 38–39: From *Beautiful Blackbird*
p. 40: Islesford Congregational Church, Maine; photograph of seagulls by C. Meis
p. 41: Drawings of Pablo Casals's festival; Pablo Casals's letter of thanks for my hand-illuminated manuscript to *The Song of the Birds*.
Translated from the French, it reads, in full:

5 June 1953

Dear Mr. Bryan,

Your words and that exquisite piece inspired by "The Song of the Birds" ("El cant dels ocells") touched me profoundly.
From the heart, I thank you. How happy I am to possess this jewel that comes to me from your sentiment, of your admirable art.
Will I have the pleasure of your presence at the 4th Festival? Without modesty I tell you that it will be very beautiful.

In affection and recognition,

Pau Casals
Prades (P. O.)

p. 42: Garden painting, *detail*
pp. 42–43: St. Gauden's Medal for Fine Draughtsmanship, awarded in 1936
p. 43: Fresco, South Solon Free Meeting House, Maine, 1956
pp. 44–45: From *Let It Shine*
p. 46: Children visiting Cranberry Isles
p. 47: Pen-and-ink drawing; drawing, both made at age fourteen
p. 48: Me, on a school visit (*inset*)
p. 49: Block-print border design
p. 50: Garden painting, *detail*
p. 51: Painting in the garden
pp. 52–53: My book covers
p. 54: Family house in Antigua, West Indies; my sister Elaine on verandah
p. 56: Interior of my home